BLAST OFF!
VENUS

D0537957

Helen and David Orme

Copyright © ticktock Entertainment Ltd 2007
First published in Great Britain in 2006 by ticktock Media Ltd.,
Unit 2, Orchard Business Centre, North Farm Road,
Tunbridge Wells, Kent, TN2 3XF

ticktock project editor: Julia Adams
ticktock project designer: Emma Randall

We would like to thank: Sandra Voss, Tim Bones, James Powell,
Indexing Specialists (UK) Ltd.

ISBN 978 1 84696 050 5
Printed in China
A CIP catalogue record for this book is available from the British Library.

Picture credits
t=top, b=bottom, c=centre, l-left, r=right, bg=background

Bridgeman Art Library: 15b; ESA: 1br, 21, 22, 23tl; NASA: front cover, 1tl, 7tr, 7bl, 13tl, 18tl, 18br, 20tl, 20tl (inset), 20br; Science
Photo Library: 4/5bg (original); Shutterstock: 2/3bg, 7tl, 11tl, 11cr, 13tr, 16bl, 23br, 24bg; ticktock picture archive: 6, 6bg, 8bl,
8cr, 9, 10bg, 10, 11b, 12c, 13bl, 14, 14bg, 15tl, 16tr, 16br, 17tr, 17bl, 18bg, 19tr, 19bl, 20br (inset), 22bg

Every effort has been made to trace the copyright holders, and we apologise in advance for any unintentional omissions.
We would be pleased to insert the appropriate acknowledgements in any subsequent edition of this publication.

Contents

Where is Venus?

There are eight planets in our **solar system**. The planets travel around the Sun. Venus is the second closest planet to the Sun.

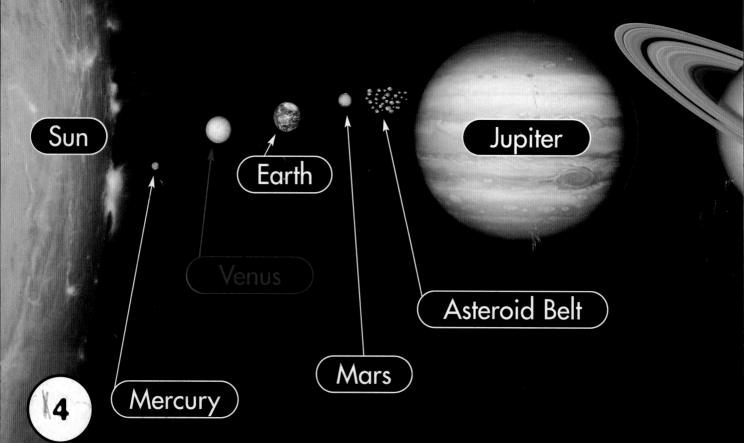

Sun

Earth

Jupiter

Venus

Asteroid Belt

Mars

Mercury

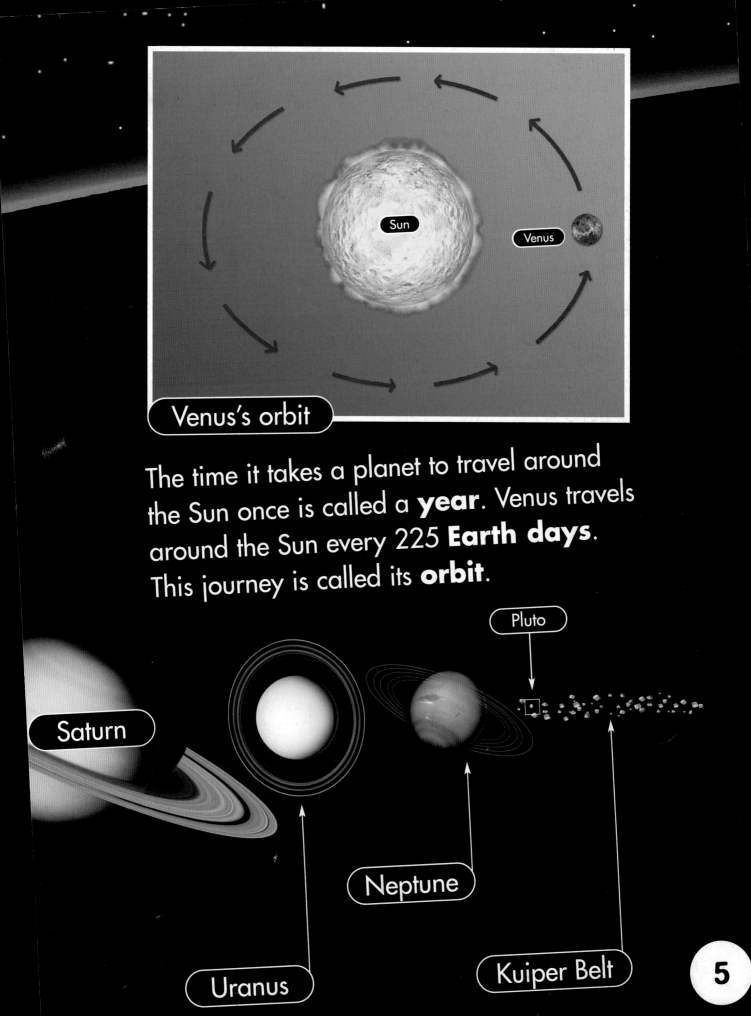

Sun

Venus

Venus's orbit

The time it takes a planet to travel around the Sun once is called a **year**. Venus travels around the Sun every 225 **Earth days**. This journey is called its **orbit**.

Pluto

Saturn

Neptune

Uranus

Kuiper Belt

Planet Facts

Venus is a very hot planet. It is covered in very thick clouds. We cannot see through these clouds with a telescope. But space probes have taken pictures of the surface.

This is a drawing of Venus's surface. It is mostly flat and very dry. There is no water on Venus.

| Earth | Venus |
| 12,756 kilometres | 12,103 kilometres |

Venus is almost the same size as Earth.
That's why it is sometimes called Earth's twin.

Planets are always spinning. A day is the time it takes a planet to spin around once. A day on Venus is 243 **Earth days** long!

Venus spins in the opposite direction of Earth.

Venus is the hottest of all the planets. It is hotter than the planet Mercury, even though Mercury is closer to the Sun.

480°C

The top temperature on Venus is about 480°C!

450°C

400°C

350°C

The highest temperature on Mercury is about 430°C.

300°C

250°C

200°C

The highest temperature measured on Earth is 58°C .

150°C

100°C

The temperature when water freezes on Earth is 0° Celsius.

50°C

0°C

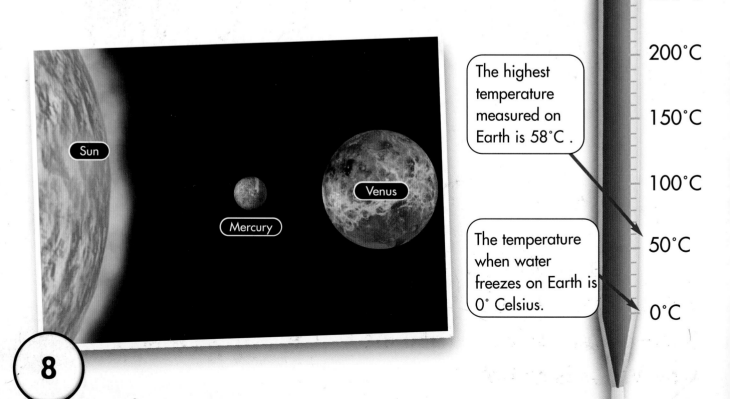

Sun

Mercury

Venus

The **atmosphere** on Venus is very thick and heavy.
This is why there is a lot of pressure on the surface.
The pressure on Venus would crush you immediately!

atmosphere

heat waves

surface of Venus

This picture shows Venus's heavy and thick atmosphere.
It stops heat escaping from the planet's surface. This is
why Venus is so hot.

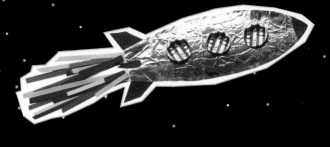

Global Warming

The **atmosphere** on Venus is mostly made of a gas called **carbon dioxide**. This gas stops nearly all of the heat on Venus from escaping into space. People worry that Earth may become like Venus.

Sun

The heat from the Sun reaches Venus's surface.

Venus

atmosphere

The thick atmosphere stops it escaping, so the planet can never cool down.

On Earth, we make a lot of carbon dioxide. We make it when we burn oil or coal. Cars, factories and planes all make this gas.

The gas gets trapped in the Earth's atmosphere. It stops heat escaping from Earth. We call this **global warming**.

Could the Earth end up hot and dry like Venus?

Earth today ● ● ● ● ● ● ● ● ● ● ● ● Earth in future?

Space probes
use machines to discover what is under the clouds of Venus. They are able to tell scientists a lot about the planet's surface.

Scientists have used the information collected by space probes to make special maps of the planet.

This is a picture of Venus that scientists have made. They use different colours for different areas on the planet.

brown means a very high mountain

yellow means a very low valley

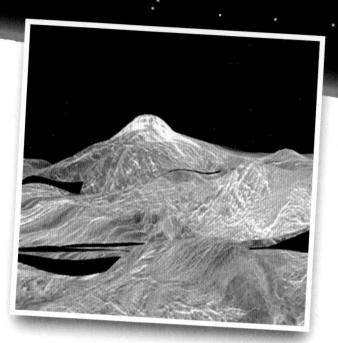

The highest mountain on Venus is called Maxwell Montes. It is about 11 kilometres high.

The highest mountain on Earth is Mount Everest in the Himalayas. It is about almost 9 kilometres high.

There may still be **active volcanoes** on Venus. Volcanoes are mountains where the hot, liquid inside of a planet bursts to the surface.

13

Finding Venus

Venus is the brightest of all the planets. It is brighter than any star in the sky. People have always wondered about Venus.

Venus was named after an ancient Roman goddess. Venus was the goddess of love and beauty.

The planet was named Venus because it was a beautiful sight shining in the morning and evening sky.

Thousands of years ago, people could see Venus even though they didn't have telescopes or binoculars. These people are using instruments to work out the position of the planets.

What Can We See?

Venus is the easiest planet to see from Earth because it is so bright. You can often see Venus when the sky is still quite light.

Look for Venus in the early morning...

Even with a telescope you can't see details of the planet's surface, because of the thick clouds.

...or in the evening.

When Venus passes in front of the Sun, the planet looks like a black dot to us.

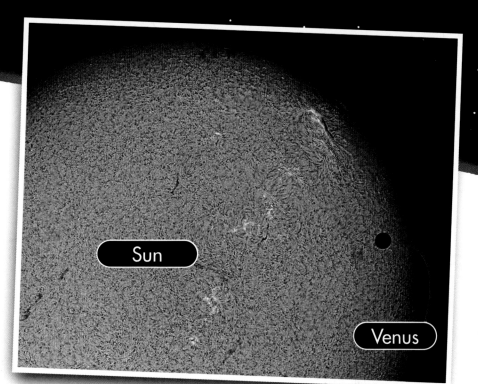

Sun

Venus

This is the telescope that was used to take the picture of Venus in front of the Sun. It is a very special telescope. It protects the scientists' eyes from the Sun.

40 inches (1m)

Warning
NEVER look directly at the Sun. It can blind you!

Venus Discoveries

Telescopes can't see through the thick clouds of Venus. Scientists have had to find other ways to study the planet.

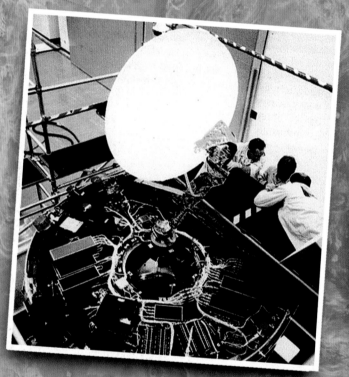

Scientists use **space probes**, like this one, to find out more about far-away planets. This is a photo of the Pioneer **orbiter**. It was sent to Venus in 1978.

This is a painting of the Pioneer orbiter above Venus. It was controlled from Earth and had 17 machines to study the temperature of Venus and its surface.

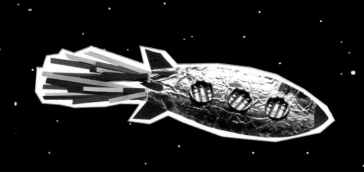

Space probes like Magellan use **radar**. Radar sends special radio waves that bounce off parts of the planet. It can help make a 3-D map of all the mountains and valleys on Venus, like this one.

This special 3-D map was also made using radar. It shows Venus and all its mountains and valleys.

Missions to Venus

There have been many space missions to Venus. Some **space probes** have even landed on the planet. The early Venus space probes were crushed by the **atmosphere.**

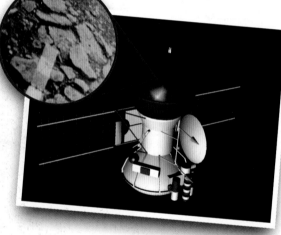

This is the Venera 9 **lander**. This Russian lander reached Venus in 1975. It was the first lander to take pictures from the surface of the planet. After sending the pictures to Earth for 50 minutes, it was destroyed by the heat on Venus!

The U.S. Magellan mission was launched in 1989. Magellan went into **orbit** round the planet to make a map of Venus.

This is the launch of Venus Express in 2005 by the European Space Agency. It arrived at Venus in April 2006 and started orbiting it. With its help, scientists are trying to find out more about the atmosphere of Venus.

New Missions

Venus is too dangerous for people because it is so hot and has such a thick and heavy **atmosphere**. If we want to explore the surface in future, it will have to be done by robots.

The robots will be controlled by scientists from Earth.

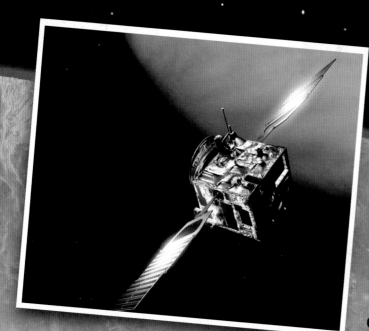

This is a painting of Venus Express **orbiting** Venus.

In the future, scientists would like to send a mission to study more of Venus's atmosphere.

Usually, scientists look for **microbes**. Some kinds of these tiny forms of life are found in the Earth's atmosphere.

If microbes like the ones in Earth's atmosphere are found in the atmosphere of another planet, life there might be possible!

Glossary

Active volcano A volcano that is still erupting.

Asteroid A rocky object that orbits the Sun. Most asteroids orbit the Sun between Earth and Mars.

Atmosphere The gases that surround a star, planet or moon.

Carbon dioxide A gas that is made when something burns.

Earth day A day is the time it takes a planet to spin around once. A day on Earth is 24 hours long.

Global warming The warming up of a planet.

This happens when gases do not let heat escape from that planet.

Lander A spacecraft designed to land on a planet or moon.

Microbes Tiny living things such as a virus or bacterium.

Orbit The path planets or other objects take around the Sun, or satellites take around planets.

Orbiter A spacecraft designed to go into orbit around a planet. It takes pictures of the planet and sends them back to Earth.

Radar A tool to help find out about the surface of a planet that is very far away. This is how scientists find out about mountains and valleys are on the surface of a planet.

Solar system The Sun and everything that is in orbit around it.

Space probe A spacecraft sent from Earth to explore the solar system. It can collect samples and take pictures.

Year The time it takes a planet to orbit the Sun.

Index